Dedicated to Samuel

This is a book about the DINOSAURS...

Dinosaurs lived over 200 million years ago.

Dinosaurs thrived in continents all over the earth...

Some even didn't mind the snow!

Dinosaurs ate a lot of different foods...

Plants...

And meat...

For some dinosaurs both items were on the menu!

menu

Insects
Plants

Imagine being a giant dinosaur...

Wandering around every day looking for a bite to eat!

With brilliant eyesight and a strong sense of smell...

It wouldn't take long before they found some delicious treats!

One thing really surprised me though...

Something I hadn't heard before...

WHAT?

Dinosaurs didn't have a voicebox...

Which means Dinosaurs couldn't roar!

So, guess what we can do?

JUMP JUMP JUMP

AND ROAR

FOR THE DINOSAURS!

Dinosaur babies were called HATCHLINGS...

Like other reptiles their young were born from eggs...

It would have been fun to watch them breaking out...

And wiggling their little Dinosaur legs!

Some dinosaurs had scales on their skin...

Perhaps like alligators
or crocodiles...

Others had fur...some had feathers...

With over fifty teeth they must've had quite a smile!

AND NOW IT'S TIME TO JUMP JUMP JUMP

AND ROAR...

FOR THE DINOSAURS!

The dinosaur diet...

Made them fart a lot
for various reasons...

But as the farty fumes rose up into the air...

It would keep them warm through all seasons!

And now it's time to...

JUMP JUMP JUMP

AND ROAR

FOR THE DINOSAURS!

WE

HELPING
THE DINOSAURS
ROAR!

Jump Series:

Jump Like a Caribou!
Jump Like a Kangaroo!
Jump at the Zoo!
Jump and Say P.U.!
Jump and Say Boo!
Jump and Say Valentine's Day Is
For Kids Too!
Jump and Look For a Clue!
Jump and Say Happy Birthday to You!
Jump For Everything Blue!
Jump, Hop and Say Happy Easter To You!
Jump and Say Cock-A-Doodle-Do!
Jump and Sing Da-Do-Do-Do!
Jump and Ask Who? Who?
Jump and Squawk Like a Cockatoo!
Jump and Ask Is It You or Ewe?
Jump and Say There's an Ewww in My
Stew!
Jump and Say Merry Christmas To You!
Jump and Cheer Happy New Year!
Jump and Say There's a Moo-Moo in a
Tutu!
Jump and Say There's a Hare in My Hair!
Jump and Say My Aunt Ate An Ant!

Jump and Say There's An Aardvark In The Amusement Park!
Jump and Buzz Like A Bee!

Clap For Series
Clap for 1!
Clap for 2!
Clap for 3!
Clap for 4!
Clap for 5!
Clap for 6!
Clap for 7!
Clap for 8!
Clap for 9!
Clap for 10!

The Cat Who Said Hello
The Three Boulders
Billy Shakespeare
Billie Shakespeare
Learn To Draw With Symmetry
ABC More Learn to Draw With Symmetry

Non-Fiction
103 Fundraising Ideas For Parent Volunteers
With Schools and Teams